AF480263

DANCES OF NORWAY

Plate I   Numedal

DANCES *of* NORWAY

KLARA SEMB

NOVERRE PRESS

ILLUSTRATED BY
PAMELA WOODS
ASSISTANT EDITOR
YVONNE MOYSE

First published in 1951
This edition published in 2021 by
The Noverre Press
Southwold House
Isington Road
Binsted
Hampshire
GU34 4PH

ISBN 978-1-914311-09-3

CONTENTS

Illustrations in Colour, pages 2, 12, 29, 39

Map of Norway, page 6

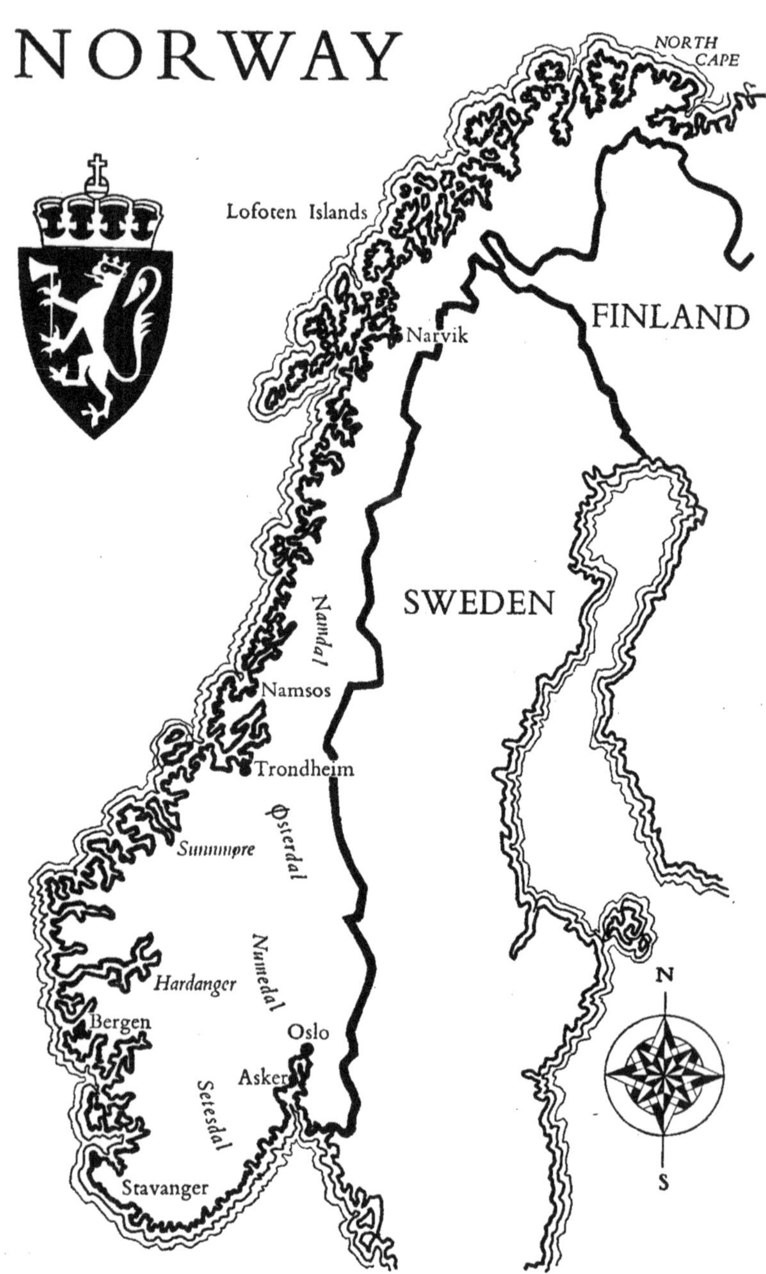

NORWAY
NORTH CAPE
Lofoten Islands
FINLAND
Narvik
Namdal
SWEDEN
Namsos
Trondheim
Østerdal
Summøre
Numedal
Hardanger
Bergen
Oslo
Asker
Setesdal
Stavanger
N
S

INTRODUCTION

Norway is a land of fjords, mountains and valleys, but also a land of rivers, lakes and forests. The scenery, now wild and terrible, now gentle, has left its mark on the inhabitants, on their songs as well as on their dances.

Our old Norse literature consisted of Edda-kvæde, Eddic poems; later the Skalds or bards found themes in sagas and lays, using alliteration and reciting their poems at feasts before kings and chieftains. Nothing, however, suggests that either song or dance was attached to these spoken verses, though, in form, there are certain points of resemblance between these skaldic poems and our oldest dance ballads. The real song-dance came with the ballad, or what in England and France became the Carole, known all over Western Europe in Court, castle and village. Icelandic sources give us some information from as early as 1119 about this medieval dance form and we may suppose that it reached Norway about the same time or a little earlier. The age of chivalry created good conditions for this artistic, polite form in which both sexes could take part and which either a man or a woman might lead; as it grew in popularity the reign of the old skald and the reciter of sagas came to an end.

Through the song-dance our ballads won a popularity no other poetry has gained. Alliteration was dropped, rhymes took its place and lyrical stanzas became a vehicle for dance.

These might contain an invitation to join the dance or some description of the dance, or a warning that disapproving eyes were on the chain:

> *At home for eight years Olaf sat*
> *(Don't tread too near me!)*
> *Ere his Mother him would see;*
> *On the grassy plain dances my maiden.*

Our epic poems developed into more polished lyrical stanzas; then the lyrical verse was forgotten, all but the burden or refrain. And it was this form of song-dance, circling to the refrain, which ever grew in popularity; in winter it was danced in the log houses, in summer in the open air, and many of our ballads sing of the dance in the light summer night of the North:

> *Step lightly over the green field;*
> *There is no daylight yet.*

At the great Midsummer festival celebrating the summer solstice people danced all through the dusk of the night. Blazing fires glowed from the hills against the twilight of the June night, while dancers moved in big circles singing their epic poems and their lyrical verses of love. Another great occasion was the Olsok Festival held in remembrance of Olaf, Saint and King, who introduced Christianity into pagan Norway and who fell at Stiklestad on July 29th, 1030.

BALLAD DANCES

Ballad subjects often travelled from country to country. For instance, one famous mystic Norwegian ballad, Draum-kvædet, seems a parallel to Dante's *Divina Commedia*, vividly describing a journey to the other world.

Peculiar to Norway are the ballads telling of fights with the Trolls, those dwarf-like beings generally hostile to humanity, living in mountains and hills. Our great mountain barriers with their far-scattered population naturally favoured the retention of superstitions and beliefs remaining from heathen times, and these continued long after the introduction of the Christian faith. Other ballads tell of the lives of giants, hero warriors and human knights; then, too, we get historical incidents and ballads about animals which are akin to fairy tales.

The Middle Ages was the great period for both ballad and folk tunes, and by degrees our folk dance, influenced by these, acquired its national character. Song-dance became dramatic, a strong element in popular custom. It lived until about 1600; in Iceland and Shetland (peopled chiefly by Norsemen) until a hundred years later, while in the Faroe Islands* it has never been forgotten, and the Chain circles and the ballads are sung as of old.

Here are a few of our ballad dances, all of which are danced again since the revival in Norwegian dancing was set on foot.

Draumkvædet, dating from the thirteenth century, has already been mentioned. It is perhaps the greatest of all our ballads, Norwegian medieval poetry at its height. When danced, four different melodies are used, to suit the verses sung. The dance itself is complicated and spectacular.

Aasmund Frægdegjæva is the story of a hero fighting the Trolls. The Trolls lived far to the north where, according to popular belief, there was a great bay, the Trollebotn. To this *Ultima Thule* Aasmund went to save the King's daughter.

Bendik and Aarolilja is a famous love story. The ballad has been translated for this handbook.

Margit Hjukse is the story of a girl spirited off into the mountains. The church bells call her home, but soon she has to return to her bewitchment. There are several other ballads dealing with this theme—Liti Kjersti for instance.

Haugebonden tells of a farmer, and a fairy belonging to the family of the English Robin Goodfellow.

* See *Dances of Denmark* in this series.

Gudmund and Signeliti is one of many ballads about the river sprites. These sometimes malevolent beings lured Signeliti into the water, whence Gudmund saved her by his beautiful music.

Falkvor Lomansson is an historical ballad to which is danced the famous Norwegian Torch Dance. The women carry small garlands of flowers which gently loop between their two hands, the men blazing torches beneath which the women pass.

Olav Liljukrans is another well-known ballad about elves; we also know the transmigration of souls as a ballad theme, and amongst our ancient riches we find a version of the widespread tragedy of the Two Sisters, equally well known in the British Isles:—

> *The youngest stood upon a stane,*
> *The eldest came and pushed her in . . .*

But the Scottish harper with us becomes two Angels from Paradise, and when the harp, made of 'her white breast-bone' and strung with 'three strands of her golden hair', has revealed the elder sister's infamy, the Angels break up the mysterious instrument and the fair young sister rises alive from its ruin.

NEW DANCES ARRIVE

Why did the song-dance at last perish in our country? Chiefly because, the answer seems to be, it was supplanted by a new form and became old-fashioned and so neglected. Scandinavian mercenaries returning from the wars in Poland and elsewhere brought home to Sweden and Finland as to Norway new dances—the Polsdansar, Polish dances.* And with these came the fiddle. These innovations did not reach the western islands for a long time, but on the mainland the old forms perished. For a while there

* See *Dances of Sweden* and *Dances of Finland* in this series.

was conflict between new and old, till out of the new
another style of dancing emerged, built partly on the Polish
dances yet still bearing the mark of the old ballad form in
rhythm. This kind of hybrid shows its peculiarities in the
deep valleys and fjord regions. Some of these dances, the
Springar, the Gangar, the Halling, the Pols and the Vosserull, are the most interesting in Norway today, at least as
regards their music. Each rural district treasures its special
form and the rhythm is peculiar to the locality. They
remain distinct owing to scarcity of communications.

With one exception these dances are pair dances—the
form which came in from the Continent—and somewhat
complicated. In a Springar there are up to nine different
steps, giving opportunity for each dancer to show off his
individual accomplishments. The man must exhibit his
virility and strength, the girl her feminine grace. Springar
music is syncopated and shows other peculiarities, for al-
though it is invariably in 3/4 time, the steps of the dancers
count 2/4, 4/4 and 3/4—with syncopated phrases in
between. Often, too, man and girl must perform different
steps to the same music. The leader gives the signal for
a change of figure by stamping or clapping his hands. The
dancers only follow his command when they are ready to
do so ; thus the figures are not dependent on a definite
number of bars. There is also a dramatic Springar in 2/4
for one man with two partners.

The Gangar is danced in two districts, Telemark and
Setesdal. That from Setesdal is perhaps the most stylised of
our Norwegian dances—an aristocratic and polite dance.

The most vigorous—indeed acrobatic—dance is certainly
the Halling, by men only, who show off before a girl, or
dance alone. Sometimes the girl holds a stick with a hat on
the end of it, herself mounted on a chair or a stone. The
agile man must, with a turning leap, kick the hat from the
stick—all to exact rhythm. The Pols and the Vosserull, like
the Springar and Gangar, are pair dances.

Plate 2   Voss.   (Details of bridal costume: Hardanger)

Figure dances seem to have reached Norway and the other northern countries about 1500, brought by English clerks who crossed the North Sea to visit our Bishops and who were by no means afraid of dancing. We now possess many, amongst them a three-handed miming reel with a happy ending, and other amusing reels. Later came the progressive dances with deep reverences and later again the ubiquitous Quadrille and the lively pair dances such as the Polka. Acclimatised, the Country dance which went from England to France and back again has, here in Norway, become graceful, spirited and speedy—modified, perhaps transformed, to Norwegian taste and spirit. Some of these Country dances have retained their original names if nothing else; many more developed wholly in Norway. The countless tunes for these forms prove their immense popularity.

✲ MUSIC ✲

The nineteenth century brought a ferment, and eventually new life, to Norwegian national culture. Collectors of ballads and folklore in general began their work, finding rich treasure, until then almost unknown, in deep valleys and remote places. The first great collector was Lindeman (1812–89) who journeyed from parish to parish noting folk tunes, especially from village fiddlers. He saved 1500 melodies for us and showed the way to others. Since then our composers have been influenced and inspired by their own Norwegian folk music. In Grieg's works it shows itself freely and unashamed. Our Norwegian hymn-book, too, is influenced and contains some forty folk tunes.

Our oldest instrument is the lur, a wind instrument of wood and birch bark made by shepherds. This has a long ancestry, coming to us from the Bronze Age, when it was made of that metal. The shepherds' lur may still be heard in mountain valleys. If fire or other danger threatens an outlying farm, the sound of the lur brings helpers from the village. The willow pipe without holes is another home-made instrument, as is the prillarhorn or goat-horn with finger-holes. Better known is the langeleik, dating from about 1500, which has a long case with a sounding board. It is laid on a table, and its 2 to 7 strings, with a melody string in the lid, are plucked with a plectrum. Moreover, the fairies played the langeleik, as we all know. The Hardanger fiddle is well known, dating from the eighteenth century only. This type of fiddle has four sympathetic under-strings which give a drone vibration. Double, even treble, stopping is used with wonderful polyphonic effect.

The Hardanger fiddlers are the repositories of our folk tunes and are in their glory at a wedding. They accompany the bridal pair to church and back and must be ready to play for three days, never tiring. The best-known fiddlers are outstanding teachers; thus their dance tunes are in no danger of being forgotten. They have their organisation, Landslaget for Spelmenn, with annual competitions for fiddlers—both Hardanger and ordinary instruments—and langeleik players.

COSTUME

Like the ballads and folk tunes our regional costumes reflect Norwegian character and temperament. They date chiefly from the Renaissance, but have been influenced by Baroque and Empire styles, which nevertheless have fused into an harmonious whole.

They vary from district to district, showing a wonderful variety. In Hardanger and other western regions the em-broidesy is marvellous; white on white, black on white, beads embroidered on scarlet cloth. Beautiful designs are worked, without a traced pattern, on fine linen. Drawn-thread work and Renaissance lace designs are beautifully done.

Sunnmöre on the west coast shows wool embroidery on wool. The dress is dark blue or black, the head-covering sometimes white with fine black embroidery; the pocket may be attached to the belt by a chased silver hook.

Coloured wool embroidery belongs to central and eastern districts; in Telemark, Baroque acanthus leaves are the chief motif and new designs are constantly created, though traditional technique is still in use.

South Norway shows home-made rucked skirts, in Setesdal very short. A remarkable part of the women's festival dress is a white petticoat with black ribbon round the hem, which is longer than the skirt.

The Lapps have their own festival dresses and every district all over the country exacts strict adherence to the local style. There have always been different costumes for weekdays and holidays. Mourning colours are white and violet. Brides used to wear a silver bridal crown, exchanging this on the second day after the wedding for the 'skaut' of the married women.

Men, too, have had their fashions from the Middle Ages, boasting beautiful embroideries and bright waistcoats differing from the rest of the suit. One of the most distinguished Telemark costumes is a black-and-white one, with black embroidery on the white cloth.

Women's dress is set off by beautiful silver brooches and clasps, and both men and women wear buckled shoes.

Norwegian costume, which varies from valley to valley, has largely been revived, as have the dances. It therefore seemed advisable to choose older, authentic costumes for our illustrations rather than those from particular danceplaces. Present-day dancers wear the dress of their own valley or region for whatever dances they are performing; and this is especially so for Bendik and Aarolilja, which is a composed dance.

About half a century ago, Hulda Garborg, the Norwegian authoress, went to the Faroe Islands to study the old Chain dance accompanied by sung ballads. With this living tradition as a model she began to revive Norwegian song-dances, retaining the fundamental six beats of the Faroe step though adding new movements. She composed dances to traditional ballads and is the founder of the present folk-dance revival. Others followed in her footsteps, amongst them the author of this handbook, who travelled the country for more than forty years teaching thousands of young people revived and living dances.

In recent times folk dancing has been connected with the big Youth Society, Noregs Ungdomslag, with more than 60,000 members and 1262 regional branches.

Annual folk-dance festivals are held at the time of the General Assembly of Noregs Ungdomslag.

Information from Noregs Ungdomslag, Prinsensgt. 6, Oslo.

THE DANCES

TECHNICAL EDITORS
MURIEL WEBSTER AND KATHLEEN P. TUCK

ABBREVIATIONS
USED IN DESCRIPTION OF STEPS AND DANCES

r—right ⎫ referring to   R—right ⎫ describing turns or
l—left   ⎭ hand, foot, etc.   L—left   ⎭ ground pattern
C—clockwise   C-C—counter-clockwise

For description of foot positions and explanations of any ballet terms the following books are suggested for reference:

A Primer of Classical Ballet (Cecchetti method). Cyril Beaumont.

First Steps (R.A.D.). Ruth French and Felix Demery.

The Ballet Lover's Pocket Book. Kay Ambrose.

Reference books for description of figures:

The Scottish Country Dance Society's Publications. Many volumes, from Thornhill, Cairnmuir Road, Edinburgh 12.

The English Folk Dance and Song Society's Publications. Cecil Sharp House, 2 Regent's Park Road, London, N.W.1.

The Country Dance Book I–VI. Cecil J. Sharp. Novello & Co., London.

The body and head should be held erect unless stated otherwise; the manner of dancing is simple and unaffected, the dancers changing their mood to fit that suggested by the music or the mime.

When standing alone, the men have the l hand rather low on the hip with the fingers forward, and the r hand hanging loosely by the side. The women hold their skirts out wide to the side.

Pair Dancing

A. As in Spring Pols. Partners face each other, the man taking the woman's l hand in his r. The joined hands are raised a little above shoulder height and lifted sideways so that they are backward as the couple move forward C-C.

B. As in Spring Pols. Partners face each other with r hand (which is passed under partner's l arm) placed on partner's l shoulder-blade. With their l hand each grasps round partner's r upper arm.

Ring Dancing

A. As in Aattetur. Chain grasp in circles of 8, men's hands below. The joined hands are then raised a little above shoulder height to form and show the ring formation.

B. As in Bendik and Aarolilja.

BASIC STEPS

Faroe Step (as in Bendik and Aarolilja). 4/4 time.	Beats
Step forward on l foot.	1
Close r foot to l foot.	2
Step forward on l foot.	3
Close r foot to side of l foot (on toe).	4

Step forward on r foot.

Close l foot to side of r foot without changing weight.

Repeat by stepping forward again on l foot, etc.

N.B.—Each Faroe step takes 1½ bars of music (6 beats).

Lilting Step (as in Aattetur). 3/4 time.
After taking a short preliminary step from the l foot, step on to r foot, at the same time bending r knee.
While lilting on r leg (softly stretching r knee and raising r heel) swing the l leg forward with a straight ankle and slightly bent knee, with the toe skimming along the ground before it is raised. (This step should be danced with a soft lilt—*not* a hop—on the standing leg, and good use made of the soft bending and stretching of this knee.)
The raised leg is only slightly bent.

Change Step (as in Seierstad Hopsa). 2/4 time.
Step forward on l foot.
Close r foot to l foot.
Step forward on l foot.
Hop on l foot.
Repeat, beginning on r foot. (1 bar.)

Pols Step (as in Spring Pols). 3/4 time.
This step is used when couples are turning together C and at the same time moving C-C round the room as in an old-fashioned Waltz. The step is similar to that used in the Viennese Waltz of the ballroom.

    Step forward r foot (small but strong step), turning to R with body.   **I**

    Step forward and round partner with l foot, still turning C.   **2**

    Place r foot on toe beside l foot, bending knees a little and lowering heels.   **3**
(Man has now made one complete turn C as well as progressing C-C round the room.)
The knees are straightened quickly as he steps forward on r foot to repeat the step.

WOMAN'S STEP

    Her step is the same as the man's but she starts with the step the man takes on beat 2.

    Step a little backward on l foot, turning C.   **I**

    Place r foot on toe beside l foot, bending the knees a little and lowering the heels.   **2**

    Small step forward on r foot.   **3**

N.B.—The rhythm of the Pols step may feel strange at first, the man's feet being joined on beat 3 and the woman's on beat 2 of the music. When the step becomes familiar this makes the rhythm most interesting.

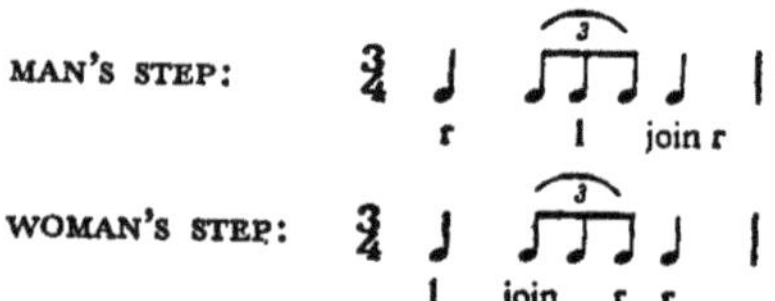

Dal Step (as in Spring Pols).
    This is very like the Lilting step but is taken with a hop instead of a lilt.

AATTETUR

Region   Asker.

Character   Quiet.

Formation   Four couples in a ring. Chain grasp, with the man's hands underneath and the woman's hands placed lightly from above. The joined hands are raised a little above shoulder height with the arms half extended. (Women stand on R of partner.) The poise of the body is a little backward, and dancers lean into the circle.

Dance	MUSIC *Bars*
FIGURE I	A
Starting l foot, take 8 Lilting steps (1 to each bar) travelling C in a ring. Turn on the 8th	1–8
bar to repeat 8 Lilting steps C-C in a ring; end facing partner in a ring.	1–8
FIGURE II: THE CHAIN. (Lilting steps.)	B
a Grand chain, giving r hands to partner, l to next dancer and so on, to meet partner half-way round on 6th step. Hands a little above shoulder height.	9–14
Change places with partner, lifting the joined r hands high to make an arch in order to look at one another. Man l hand on hip, woman holds dress.	15–16
Release hands and chain back to meet partner. Men now face C and women C-C.	9–16

21

AATTETUR

Allegretto (♩. = 6o)
Arranged by Arnold Foster
A
1
2
3
4
5
6
7
8
(8)
1
2
B
9
10
11
12
13
14
15
16
(16)
1
2

b Honour partner. Man folds his arms over the chest and bends his back and his head. The woman holds her skirt out wide to the side and, stepping on to the r foot, makes a deep curtsey, keeping the back nearly straight and bending the head deeply. The woman's l knee should touch the floor, after which she rises slowly, keeping her head down as long as possible.

c Couples dance together, turning C and moving round the room C-C with 10 old-fashioned Waltz steps. Man has his hands on the woman's hips, while she places her hands on his shoulders.

Man then swings his partner over to his r side, supporting her with his r arm, and he dances on the spot. Woman releases her r hand and moves across in front of the man, allowing her l hand to slip down the man's r arm until they clasp hands.

Repeat movements of bars 17–32.

	C 17–20
	21–30
	31–32
	17–32

BENDIK AND AAROLILJA

Origin	A traditional ballad from the Middle Ages. The dance movements were arranged by the author about forty years ago.
Character	Song dance, the mood changing to fit the dramatic events.
Formation	Any number of couples in a circle moving C. Each dancer's r hand is on top and l hand under those of the dancers on either side. The joined hands are then raised so that the arms are close to the body, elbows down.
Tempo	The speed of the movements is increased or diminished according to the dramatic events sung. In this ballad the first half of the 1st and 2nd verses is danced in a moderately lively tempo and the second part of each at a slower speed. The 3rd and 4th verses are in a vigorous rhythm; the 5th and 6th verses are taken passionately but in a slower tempo, and the last two verses very slowly. There is no movement between the verses.

Dance	MUSIC
FIRST VERSE	*Bars*
a Moving C in a ring, dance 4 Faroe steps and four beats of the 5th; then turn to face the centre of the circle.	1–7
Women take a small step towards the centre on the r foot and then place it by the side of the l foot on the 2nd beat. The	8 (beats 1, 2)

men step in farther than the women and join hands; they stand on the r foot.

b Men bend the knee a little and straighten it as they step back on the l foot, at the same time lifting the arms forward and upward, and then softly down as they close the r to the l foot.
At the same time the women, bending their knee and bowing the head, take a step inward passing under the men's arms, then join hands and raise the head as they place the r foot to the side of the l foot.

    8
(beats 3, 4)
    9
(beats 1, 2)

c The women now repeat the steps and movements of the men in *b*, and the men those of the women. They stand still when finished.

    9
(beats 3, 4)
10–11

VERSES 2–10

Repeat the above for the second and all other verses except the last.

1–11
repeated

LAST VERSE

a 4 full Faroe steps and four beats of the 5th, as before; then men step toward centre with r foot and place l to side of r foot, while the women take 2 steps on the spot.

1–7
8
(beats 1, 2)

b Men stand still and lift the arms, palm to palm, forward and upward while they sing the word 'Aarolilja', keeping the arms raised as they sing the last words. At the same time the women, standing close behind the men, lift the arms, crossing them on the breast and slowly lowering the head until the chin is on the hands.

    8
(beats 3, 4)
9–11

BENDIK AND AAROLILJA

This tune is arranged for practice. The dance should be performed to unaccompanied singing.

c The dancers remain thus until the last note
fades away. The men then in silence bend
a little forward and, lowering the arms,
rise quietly and slowly. When they have
finished this movement, the women slowly
lower their arms and raise the head.

The movement represents a lily opening
and closing.

BENDIK AND AAROLILJA

Bendik rode to Sölondo,
There a maid to find,
But never will he ride back again:
Cruel fate dooms him there to die.
  Aarolilja, why sleep you so long?

Young Bendik dwelt in the King's castle
More than a week or two;
He fell in love with the King's daughter,
Maiden so fair and true.
  Aarolilja, why sleep you so long?

The King he built a drawbridge high,
Built it of shining gold.
'Whoever crosses this bridge shall die,
Be he prince or warrior bold.'
  Aarolilja, why sleep you so long?

Answered the King young Bendik bold,
Thus boldly answered he,
'It is I who will cross your bridge of gold
E'en if I die presently.'
  Aarolilja, why sleep you so long?

Then Bendik tells her of his love,
Praises her beauty so rare:

Plate 3   Sunnmöre, and couple from Setesdal

'Like ripe yellow apples bending low
Are the braids of your golden hair.'
    Aarolilja, why sleep you so long?

Down came the fist of the Danish King:
'Now shall young Bendik die.
Not all the wealth of the wide, wide world
Pardon for him can buy.'
    Aarolilja, why sleep you so long?

Cries out the maiden to the King,
'Spare, Father, spare my love.'
'Cease, daughter, cease, ere this sword of mine
Be dripping with maiden's blood.'
    Aarolilja, why sleep you so long?

Shadows fell on the whole wide world,
All living things in their pain,
The leaves and the deer and the silent birds
Begging his life in vain.
    Aarolilja, why sleep you so long?

There beside the lonely church
Beautiful Bendik was slain:
High, high in the tower she pined and died,
Fair broken-hearted maid.
    Aarolilja, why sleep you so long?

On the north side young Bendik sleeps,
On the south Aarolilja lies,
And out of their graves two lilies grow,
Marvel to sorrowing eyes.
    Aarolilja, why sleep you so long?

High o'er the church the lilies grow,
Each to each other they cling;
A-twining together the flowers they blow,
Foretelling the doom of the King.
    Aarolilja, why sleep you so long?

SEIERSTAD HOPSA

Region   Namdal.

Character   Lively.

Formation   In two lines facing each other, men on L and
women on R if facing front. Each man has
l hand on hip, each woman holds her dress out
wide to the side. Traditionally the dance is
started by the first two couples only and finishes
when all, after dancing, reach their own place
again.

Dance	MUSIC *Bars* B
INTRODUCTION	
1st man takes 3 walks across to his partner (l, r, l), then closes r foot to l and makes a deep bow, placing his r hand on his heart. 1st woman greets her partner with a deep, slow curtsey, standing on l foot and circling the r foot behind. (This takes 2 bars.)	9–10
1st man greets 2nd woman by stepping across with his l foot, pointing the r foot, then drawing this foot to the side of the l as he makes his bow. (2 bars.)	11–12
1st man then walks 3 steps towards 2nd man, to whom he bows, still with hand to heart; and 2nd man the same. (2 bars.)	13–14
1st man finishes in his own place. (2 bars.)	15–16

A
1–4

1st and 2nd couples move down the set with 4 Change steps, joining up and turning as follows:—

1st man grasps 1st woman's r hand with his l hand.

1st man grasps 2nd woman's r hand with his r hand.

2nd man grasps his partner's l hand with his r hand.

2nd man grasps 1st woman's l hand with his l hand (under joined hands of 1st man and 2nd woman).

In this position 1st man makes a quarter-turn to the R; 1st woman makes a quarter-turn to the L; 2nd woman makes a quarter-turn to the L, to lead; 2nd man moves under the arch made by 1st man and 2nd woman and then turns to follow the 2nd woman.

5–8

1st and 2nd couples move to front of set with 4 Change steps as follows:—

1st man lifts up joined r hands and turns C to face forward.

1st woman turns under the same arch and ends on L side of her partner.

2nd woman makes half-turn to the R and stands on R of 1st man.

2nd man moves forward to end on L of 1st woman; in this position 2nd couple will have their linked arms lying behind the necks of the 1st couple.

End in own place in the line thus: 1st man pulls with his l hand so that 1st woman moves to her place passing under the arch made by the 1st man and 2nd woman.

SEIERSTAD HOPSA

Partners give r hands and all start l foot. Grand chain for 6 steps.

B
9–14

Each man swings his partner by grasping her upper arm with the l hand so that the couples change places; this means that the 2nd couple will have the larger turn and will end in the top place, 1st couple having moved down one place.

15–16

The figures are then repeated by the 1st couple with the 3rd couple, and so with each couple in turn. When the original 1st couple are making the chain with the 4th couple, the new leading couple (original 2nd couple) will dance the Introduction with the 3rd couple now standing in the second place, so they too will enter the dance.

SEIERSTAD HOPSA : alternative tune

Arranged by Arnold Foster

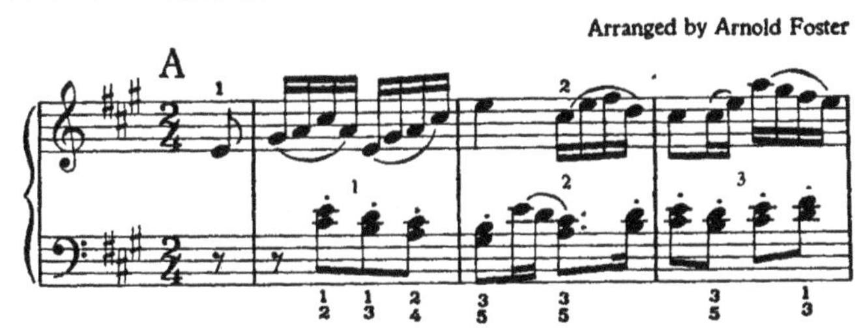

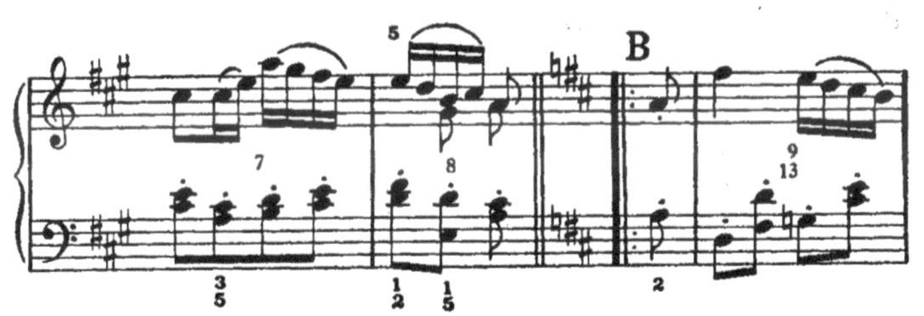

		MUSIC

Region   Österdal (forest region).

Character   Lively.

Formation   For any number of couples in a circle. Each couple turns C and moves C-C round the room.

Dance

		MUSIC *Bars*

FIGURE I

  Start facing each other, women on outside of circle. Partners join inside hands so that they are raised and stretched backward a little above shoulder height. Man starts l and woman r foot.   **A**

a 5 running steps moving C-C round the room, swinging the joined hands forward. Bring feet together on the 6th beat; then, facing partner, pass r hand under partner's l arm, laying r hand on his or her shoulder-blade, etc. (See Arm Holds, page 18: Pair Dancing, B.)   1–2

b RUNDPOLS (Round Pols). Couples dance together, turning C and moving C-C with Pols steps. Man starts r foot and will take 5 full Pols steps. Woman starts l foot backward and joins r foot to l foot (i.e. the last two beats of the step) and then starts the full step with the r foot. She will take 3 full steps.   3–7

  Loosen hold on arms and join hands, the man taking off from the r foot with an 'appell' (stamp) to leap and then land facing partner   8 (beats 1 and 2)

with feet apart; the woman taking off from the l foot to leap and then land facing partner with feet together. End with the joined hands raised sideways to shoulder level.   (beat 3) *a* With hands joined with partner's and lifted to shoulder level, dance 2 Dal steps, man swinging r and woman l leg across first.   The joined hands swing down and across to follow the line of the leg.

Face C-C and run 3 steps forward; immediately grasp for Rundpols, as in Figure I.

b RUNDPOLS with partner. This time the man will have only 4 full steps.

Finish with man swinging the woman into her place on the outside and facing him. The woman lets her l hand slide down the man's l arm until they clasp hands.

The inside, joined hands are then raised backward as in Figure I.

FIGURE III

a Swinging the joined hands downward and forward to gain impetus, slide forward on inside foot. Then let go hands and turn on the ball of this foot away from partner, and finish by hopping forward at the end of the turn on the same foot.

$$\left\{ \begin{array}{ccc} \text{Count slide,} & \text{turn,} & \text{hop} \\ \textit{Beats:} \quad 1 & 2 & 3 \end{array} \right\}$$

2 runs forward C-C, and face partner with feet together and grasp as before for Rundpols.

b RUNDPOLS. Finish as in Figure I, facing partner after the leap with an 'appell'.

N.B.—This dance is an outgrowth of the very difficult Polsdans, which is related to Springar.

The music references in the right margin are:

Figure	Section	Bars
II a	B	9–10
		11
II b		12–15
		16
III a	A	1
		2
III b		3–8

Plate 4   Telemark

BIBLIOGRAPHY

BJÖRNDAL, ARNE.—*Norske Slaattar*. (Norwegian Dance Airs.)

DREIER, J. F. L.—*Norske Folkedrakter av Einar Lexow*. Kristiania [Oslo], 1913. (Drawings of Norwegian peasant costumes from 1800.)

ELLING, CATHARINUS.—*Vore Folkemelodier*. Kristiania, 1909. (Our Folk Melodies.)

—— *Vore Kjæmpeviser*. Kristiania, 1914. (Our Hero Ballads.)

—— *Nye Bidrag till Belysning av Norsk Folkemusik*. Oslo, 1933. (New Contributions to the Study of Norwegian Folk Music.)

GARBORG, HULDA.—*Songdansen i Nordlandi*. 3rd ed. Kristiania, 1922. (The Song-Dance in Nordland.)

HEYERDAHL, A.—*Norske Danser og Slaatter*. (Norwegian Dances and Dance Airs.)

LIESTÖL, K., K. SEMB and A. SVINNDAL.—*Danseviser*. (*Norske Folkedansar*, vol. I.) 5th ed. Oslo, 1946. (Ballads and songs.)

SANDVIK, O. M.—*Folkemusik i Gudbrandsdalen*. Kristiania, 1919. (Folk Music in Gudbrandsdal.)

—— *Norsk Folkemusik*. Kristiania, 1921. (Norwegian Folk Music.)

—— *Österdals Musik*. Oslo, 1943. (Folk Music from Österdal.)

SEMB, KLARA.—*18 Norske Folkedansar*. Oslo, 1916. (18 Norwegian dance airs.)

—— *Rettleiing om Dansen*. (*Norske Folkedansar*, vol. II.) 4th ed. Oslo, 1948. (Notated folk dances with illustrations.)

—— *Slaattar*. (*Norske Folkedansar*, vol. III.) Oslo, 1925. (Dance airs.)

www.ingramcontent.com/pod-product-compliance
Lightning Source LLC
Chambersburg PA
CBHW040036070726
47636CB00071B/481